Zoo Animals

Tiger

Patricia Whitehouse

Heinemann Library
Chicago, Illinois

© 2003 Reed Educational & Professional Publishing
Published by Heinemann Library,
an imprint of Reed Educational & Professional Publishing,
Chicago, Illinois

Customer Service 888-454-2279
Visit our website at www.heinemannlibrary.com

Designed by Sue Emerson, Heinemann Library
Printed and bound in the United States by Lake Book Manufacturing, Inc.

07 06 05 04
10 9 8 7 6 5 4 3

Library of Congress Cataloging-in-Publication Data
Whitehouse, Patricia, 1958-
    Tiger / Patricia Whitehouse.
        p. cm. — (Zoo animals)
Includes index.
Summary: An introduction to tigers, including their size, diet and everyday life style, which highlights differences between those in the wild and those living in a zoo habitat.
    ISBN: 1-58810-904-6 (HC), 1-40340-648-0 (Pbk.)
    1. Tigers—Juvenile literature. [1. Tigers. 2. Zoo animals.] I. Title.
    QL737.C23 W52 2002
    599.756—dc21
                        2001007437

Acknowledgments
The author and publishers are grateful to the following for permission to reproduce copyright material:
Title page, pp. 7, 14, 18, 22, 24 Lynn M. Stone/DRK Photo; p. 4 Anup Sham/DRK Photo; pp. 5, 8, 11, 13, 15 Chicago Zoological Society/The Brookfield Zoo; p. 6 M. C. Chamberlain/DRK Photo; p. 9 Tom Brakefield/DRK Photo; p. 10 Joe McDonald/Visuals Unlimited; p. 12 E. A. Kuttapan/Naturepl.com; p. 16 Erwin and Peggy Bauer/Bruce Coleman Inc.; p. 17 SuperStock; p. 19 Konrad Wothe/Minden Pictures; p. 20 Yan Gluzberg/Visuals Unlimited; p. 21 Valmik Thapar/Peter Arnold, Inc.; p. 23 (col. 1, T-B) Chicago Zoological Society/The Brookfield Zoo, Chicago Zoological Society/The Brookfield Zoo, Jack Ballard/Visuals Unlimited; p. 23 (col. 2, T-B) Corbis, Doug Perrine/DRK Photo, Jim Schulz/Chicago Zoological Society/The Brookfield Zoo; back cover (L-R) Chicago Zoological Society/The Brookfield Zoo, Konrad Wothe/Minden Pictures

Cover photograph by Chicago Zoological Society/The Brookfield Zoo
Photo research by Bill Broyles

Special thanks to our advisory panel for their help in the preparation of this book:

Eileen Day, Preschool Teacher
Chicago, IL

Ellen Dolmetsch,
Library Media Specialist
Wilmington, DE

Kathleen Gilbert, Teacher
Round Rock, TX

Sandra Gilbert,
Library Media Specialist
Houston, TX

Angela Leeper,
Educational Consultant
North Carolina Department
of Public Instruction
Raleigh, NC

Pam McDonald, Reading Teacher
Winter Springs, FL

Melinda Murphy,
Library Media Specialist
Houston, TX

We would also like to thank Lee Haines, Assistant Director of Marketing and Public Relations at the Brookfield Zoo in Brookfield, Illinois, for his review of this book.

Some words are shown in bold, **like this.**
You can find them in the picture glossary on page 23.

Contents

What Are Tigers?

Tigers are **mammals.**

Mammals have hair or fur on their bodies.

In the wild, tigers might be hard to see.

But you can see tigers at the zoo.

What Do Tigers Look Like?

Tigers have striped hair.

Most tigers are yellow-brown with black stripes.

Each tiger's stripes look a little different.

What Do Baby Tigers Look Like?

A baby tiger looks just like its parents, but it is smaller.

A baby tiger is called a **cub**.

New cubs are about the size
of a kitten.

Where Do Tigers Live?

In the wild, some tigers live in forests.

Other tigers live in **swamps** or **grasslands**.

In the zoo, tigers live in **enclosures.**

They have a lot of room to move around.

What Do Tigers Eat?

In the wild, tigers eat big animals.

Sometimes they eat deer.

At the zoo, tigers eat meat.

Zookeepers feed them every day.

What Do Tigers Do All Day?

In the wild, tigers spend the day resting.

At the zoo, tigers sleep and play during the day.

They sleep more because they do not have to hunt.

What Do Tigers Do at Night?

In the wild, tigers hunt at night.

At the zoo, tigers sleep at night.

What Sounds Do Tigers Make?

Tigers growl, grunt, and roar.

Their roar can be heard very far away.

Some tigers have very loud roars.

Their roars can scare monkeys.

How Are Tigers Special?

Tigers are strong swimmers.

Today, not many tigers live in the wild.

Many people are trying to save them.

Quiz

Do you remember what these tiger parts are called?

Look for the answers on page 24.

? ?

Picture Glossary

cub
pages 8, 9

mammal
page 4

enclosure
page 11

swamp
page 10

grassland
page 10

zookeeper
page 13

Note to Parents and Teachers

Reading for information is an important part of a child's literacy development. Learning begins with a question about something. Help children think of themselves as investigators and researchers by encouraging their questions about the world around them. In this book, the animal is identified as a mammal. A mammal is an animal that is covered with hair or fur and that feeds its young with milk from its body. The symbol for mammal in the picture glossary is a dog nursing its babies. Point out that although the photograph for mammal shows a dog, many other animals are mammals—including humans.

Index

Answers to quiz on page 22

hair   stripes

24